THE

SILENT

DISCIPLINE

OF

DELIGHT

By

Arnold Michael

Author of

BLESSED AMONG WOMEN

BROTHERS OF THE GRAPE

Global Citizens Publishing, *Publishers*
San Clemente, California 92672, US

THOU HAST MULTIPLIED THE NATION AND NOT INCREASED THE JOY.

ISAIAH 9:3

DELIGHT THYSELF IN THE LORD; AND HE SHALL GIVE THEE THE DESIRES OF THINE HEART.

PSALM 37:4

THERE IS A PRINCIPLE WHICH IS A BOX AGAINST ALL INFORMATION, WHICH IS PROOF AGAINST ALL ARGUMENT AND WHICH CANNOT FAIL TO KEEP A MAN IN EVERLASTING IGNORANCE – THIS PRINCIPLE IS CONDEMNATION BEFORE INVESTIGATION.

HERBERT SPENCER

DEDICATIONS

Because of all the arts and sciences the art of living is the most important, the most exciting and the most rewarding, this book is dedicated to your discovery that, just as sure as you know that you are alive, you can be just as sure that you are the Power by which you can make your life whatever you want it to be. To know that you as Life can never be separated from the Power of Life and to *use* that Power to create your desired World is the Art of Living.

-Arnold Michael

This book is revised and published as one of Emily K. Michael's (who many of us affectionately called Kay) last requests. Kay was an extraordinary woman who knew the value of her husband's work and assisted him in many ways. She was a writer, teacher, and minister. Her motherhood reached out to those in prison. She nursed Arnold's former wife in their home. Her encouragement, her example, and her support were felt by many, and certainly by me! She looked beyond my faults and frailties and handed me the foundation and works of "Dr. Mike" to be shared with others. Kay, my beloved sister, it is indeed my delight to dedicate this revised edition to your memory.

-Charles Sommer

We must look at other individuals as SOULS and not beings with faults and frailties. Each soul is striving to grow and learn, whether he or she does it consciously and deliberately or subconsciously and unknowingly. Learning this really changed my attitude in so many ways, especially in human relationships.

-Emily K. Michael

ACKNOWLEDGMENTS

Many people helped make this revision possible and to those people we would like to extend heartfelt thanks. To Rev. Toni G. Boehm, Nicole Christine, Virginia Essene, Mark Avraham Libowitz, and Mag. Fj Zoder, thank you for taking the time to read and comment on the manuscript – your encouraging words were wonderful to behold. To Susan Allen at Lightning Source, your patience and flexibility helped make this revision possible. To Marci Cortese, your editing skills were greatly appreciated. And Angela Escobar, your time transcribing the original manuscript and editing this new addition was invaluable. You've all been a joy and a DELIGHT to work with. God bless!

TABLE OF CONTENTS

INTRODUCTION
To Yourself

What is the cry that has resounded from the hopeless heart down through the ages? It is – "How can I reach God?"

What is God? What else could God be except Life: your life, my life, everyone's life – the only Presence and the only Power individualized in us as our presence and our power. Therefore, since we are alive, we have already reached God because we are already one with the Life that He is.

There is a story of a small group of people in a boat who, sighting a steamer, sent out a call for help saying, "We are dying of thirst." The reply was, "Let down your buckets, you are in the mouth of the Great Amazon."

This illustrates the value of the message of Science of Mind, of metaphysics or what we call "New Thought." And that message is – We are already one with that which we seek.

In our approach to what is termed New Thought, if we do not completely understand, we will believe that our personal God is being taken away from us. But when we do understand our hearts will sing with the wonderful way God is personal to us. So personal that, when we think, we are using His faculty of thought. So personal that, when we feel, we are using His faculty of feeling. So personal that His Power automatically responds to *our* power, to every thought we think and every feeling we feel.

Could God be more personal than this, to share with us the glorious privilege of being a person? A person with our own thoughts, our own feelings and our own power, which responds to create our own world?

Just as the people in the mouth of the Amazon, we do not realize that we are already immersed in the waters of Life. Therefore the answer to the cry – "How can I reach God" is in the cry. The fact that we *can* cry is proof that we are one with God because God is the Life we have to *use* in order to cry.

Most of us are waiting for something yet to happen in our lives before we can really begin to live. We are waiting for that required strength, that needed ability, that necessary wisdom. We feel that something is lacking and we are waiting for it to be added to the gift of Life so that we can begin to experience the fullness of life. This feeling that something is lacking or lost is the origin of and what is meant by the lost word.

However, that which is lost is the truth that nothing is lost. The only thing that is to be added is the understanding that *nothing additional* is needed.

This is why the name of the lost word is I AM, for I AM is the way we define the gift of consciousness. To be able to say I AM is proof that we are alive and that we know it. This is the only lost word which means – the *loss* of the *use* of our word or the loss of our own authority of power.

Therefore, the greatest wisdom is to realize that we do not have to seek God, that *because we are alive* we are using or not using the God Power which we seek on the outside of ourselves.

If you want to use your arms or your hands, you do not have to seek God or to ask God His permission to do so. It was given to you as a functional part of the gift of life. In the same way is the Power a functional part of your being.

If we did not use our arms, we would have a sense of loss, but it would not be because we did not *use*. Automatically, even unconsciously, we command our hands and they obey us. In the same way we are to command the Power and it will obey us. The bible says it this way – "Command ye me concerning the works of my hands." This is the message brought to us by the Master Jesus and for which he was crucified for daring to say that, "He and His Father were one."

This does not mean that man is all of God, but it does mean that he is as much of God as is needed to fulfill his nature, which is *man the manifestor in his world,* of all that is necessary to make that world his dominion.

So, let us right now, no longer ask God to *be* God any more that He has already been God, and instead *use* the Power He has given us to be the god of our own personal world, the creator of our own experiences.

God's plan for us requires that we be independent of Him. How can we learn to be a creator unless we create? How can we create if we refuse to use our creative power?

Our greatest trouble comes from trying to give our power *back* to God. In an emergency we cry out to the outside God to take over instead of *using* the power already allocated to us for *just* such an emergency.

The outside God cannot take over the situation without taking away our independence – and to take away our independence takes away the function upon which our own awakening Godhood depends. Could any situation be worth this?

Our emergencies will be less and less as we use our power more and more – not just for emergencies. We must become habitually creative – habitually the deliberate director of our life in every department.

So, let's get introduced to ourselves once and for all. Let's realize that we are much more than we ever thought we were. We are truly Sons of God, which means we are created in the image of His creativity.

Not only do we have the power to function in OUR WORLD independently of God, but it is also our responsibility to ourselves and to Him – for, only as we use our God-given Power to accomplish our God-given Purpose can we glorify ourselves. And, only as we glorify ourselves do we glorify God.

So, now that we know *who* we are, let's start *being* ourselves.

PROLOGUE

– By Charles Sommer

I was first introduced to my friend, colleague, and mentor, Arnold Michael, by the inspirational book he authored, "Blessed Among Women." Little did I know then that I would carry forward the beautiful works that he initiated. When "Doctor Mike" (as he was affectionately called) made his earthly transition on the Feast Day of Our Lady of Guadalupe, the mystical baton was energetically and legally passed to me to bring forth what he taught, what he knew, and what he understood to be the "Truth of Being."

In Dr. Mike's booklet "The Discipline of Delight" is conveyed all we need to know and practice to express joy in the contentment of daily living. Our God-likeness has created the context of absolute joy and as Dr. Mike and I understand, it is the task of spiritual beings to bring forth the content of joy into our human experience.

The tendency in our human condition is to react to negative experiences in a way that stirs discontent. Within the spirit of discontent lives the Spirit of Joy for the students of truth to discover and implement. In a metaphorical sense, we bring heaven to hell. Hell often results in illness, lack of supply (necessities), unhappiness with self or others and fear which keeps us from expressing our natural

11

creativity.

Dr. Mike, in the context and content of his writing on The Discipline of Delight, gives us the tools to move from discontent to contentment, even in the face of any challenge or difficulty. In truth, we all have the tools to bring joy into every moment of now. What tools we use and the discipline we employ determine the outcome.

Emmet Fox, who I have labeled the "Grandfather of Spiritual Psychology," said: "The lingering half-beliefs in mind over matter will have given way to the knowledge and power of spiritual thought control."[1] Where we place our attention and the thought we empower with our mind and feeling does make a difference. The Master Teacher Jesus is often misunderstood by we in the Christian community who often think of him as the exception, or the only child of God, neither of which is true. Jesus is the Master Spiritual Psychologist who gave us the keys to good health, right human relationships, prosperity and creative fulfillment. In essence, he spoke of and demonstrated the importance of where we place our attention. He gave us a Universal God that is Love Itself, not a God of retribution that is based on fear, supplication, or appeasement. Ego without Love creates disease, disorder and dissention.

---

[1] Fox, Emmet. 1993 *Diagrams For Living*, San Francisco, California, HarperSanFrancisco, 229 pages, FirstHarperCollins paperback edition.

Spiritual Psychologists teach us to place our attention on God as Jesus learned to do. Our thoughts centered on God bring out our God-likeness, resulting in expressing true Love (not sentimental love), Joy, Peace, and blessed Assurance. As we learn to do this, we begin to transform our minds and to awaken to a more enlightened way of being in the world. Individuals that do this are often called: good people, light workers, children of God, peace makers, etc. Spirituality is not about Ego or Power alone. We all know what happens when power is not in balance with Love-Intelligence. The Blessed Trinity is comprised of the three in one in a perfect synthesis which I call the Spirit of God. The Spirit of God does express through all of us.

As we disciple ourselves to put God first, our egotistical tendency to put ourselves first diminishes. Of course, we often expect others to put us first and we miss the mark. Missing the mark means expressing less than our full potential. Sometimes we caregivers tend to make everyone else's needs more important than our own. Yet, there is something in us as us that can bring Ego-Love-Intelligence into a synthesis, into a balance where we light up. This is the middle path of the Buddha, or the Christ-like awareness of Jesus. If we would like to grow into this more enlightened consciousness it requires a discipline. We do not say that "The Silent Discipline of Delight" is the only way to grow in Spiritual discernment. We do say that, if you put some energy into this practice over a prolonged period, change for the better is inevitable. Whatever it is that we really desire and give our attention to is paramount to what we create in our life.

To Arnold Michael's title, "The Discipline of Delight," I have added the word "Silent." It is in the silence of our own mind that we do the work. It is in the silence where the seed of our aspirations bring forth the inspiration. Our aspirations create our inspiration. The related activities arising from our intuition are delightful. This is how our Essential Divinity works through us, as us. It brings light heartedness into our expression.

I am happy to publish this 2006 revised edition to the "Discipline of Delight." Dr. Mike's work is not changed or altered in any way. It is clear, concise, and powerful. When Dr. Mike spoke to an audience, he always brought into his deeply profound thought a keen sense of humor. When I first met Arnold he was a semi-invalid in his late seventies. On one of my visits to his home in Ojai, California, I observed he was sitting on a rubber inflated tube that looked like a large donut. I asked why and he explained to me that he had an injury to his tail bone. I asked him if his injury taught him anything. He gave me a quizzical look and with a twinkle in his eye he said, "Yes, I know how I created this injury and what it came from. When I was younger, I would get angry with someone and I would say (within the silence of my mind), 'I will kick you in the ass so hard that it will travel up to your throat.'"

We both laughed and I am happy that he took my question in the spirit in which it was intended.

I invite the reader to enter into the silence at the end of each of the four capsules and jot down any ideas, images, or feelings that arise in your consciousness. Take Delight in your expression, it is the life of God coming out of the Silence.

In conclusion, as we practice the silent disciple of delight we eventually lighten. Yes, we may fail or fall backwards. Learning anything new is awkward at first, but eventually we get better at it. The benefits of this practice will vary depending on how entrenched our negative traits are. Among these are fear, hatred, distrust, need for conquest, aggression, apathy, blame, shame, denial, and laziness. These negative traits are in the gray area of consciousness. We have enough gray matter; now let's lighten it up. Let's temper our gray matter (intellect) with compassion, genuine love and with discernment.

You are invited to read this book and use the exercises if you like. It is our delight to share it with you.

Cheers, *Charles Sommer*

THE ONLY DISCIPLINE

A Zen Buddhist monk and his student were traveling through the country, and the student asked his teacher the question, "How does man have dominion over his life?" The monk stopped and, removing his pack from his back, placed it on the ground, indicating to the student in language that he could understand that all man's burdens and limitations are unnatural states and just need to be removed. The student nodded his head comprehendingly and asked this question, "But how do we remove our burdens and limitations?"

The teacher then replaced the pack upon his back and strode down the path singing joyously, which told the student that any effort to remove our burdens must be made while the burden is still on our back, because we must start from where we already are and that there is the Power that removes man's limitations and that we activate that Power in our lives by praising and being joyful that it *is*.

It is a wonderful thing to realize that man's only discipline is a Discipline of Delight – delight in the knowledge that his freedom is his Natural State, and that delight in *this truth* activates the Power which *removes* all restrictions to his freedom.

The Bible is filled with instruction in regard to this truth, for we are constantly told, "to praise the Lord, to love the Lord, to delight in the Lord, and to make joyful noises unto the Lord." In Biblical days the Lord was synonymous with absolute Power. This Power within us is Lord, because it, too, is absolute in its ability to do what it is directed to do. It is also referred to as the Lord God, which means the Power God gave us as our Power to accomplish our Good.

All that man needs to enjoy his Natural State of health, happiness and prosperity has already been provided within the gift of Life itself. If it were not true there would be nothing that man could do to bring it about.

What is it that man can do? Since the purpose of the gift of Life is to share God's delight in life, it of necessity follows that any step we take in the direction of its fulfillment must be in accordance with this purpose. We could not make a movement in the direction of this destiny of ever increasing delight except as *some* aspect of delight be used – because it would be impossible to become delighted by being sad. Therefore, to enact the Power of our dominion, we must use delight by delighting in the Power. Thus do we increase our delight, which is Life's purpose, and at the same time we activate the Power which is designed to serve its purpose. Therefore, man's only discipline is the Discipline of Delight.

Now this sounds very wonderful and we would like to accept it and use it. First, we must get a new concept of discipline. It has long been interpreted as the overcoming of the lower nature. Such words as conquest and overcoming suggest an aggressive approach. The Discipline of Delight is not a man weary from wrestling with his lower nature, but is a poised and relaxed man achieving through realization instead of conflict – a jubilant and beholding man.

It is not a process of suffering our way into a spiritual state, but is a sense of freedom from any idea of struggle with anything within ourselves or out of ourselves. It is not an effort to kill our faults but the directing of our attention upon Good as the only Reality.

With this different concept of discipline and with our realization that our relationship with God is to share His Life and His Power by which life's goals are attained, it leaves us with only the necessity of disciplining ourselves to be delighted in our Power, which *activates it* in our life, thereby providing us with the wand of authority over our own world.

Included in the Power is the power to choose, to decide what the Power shall accomplish through us. This is not a restriction of the Power any more than the choice of the song from the available songs is a restriction of the singer's ability. Many of us know what we want, but do not realize how little we want it. How *much* do you want what you want – enough to activate the Power to let it through?

A research group conducted an experiment to find out if living things were affected by Power as thought. Two seeds were planted in the same box of earth and given equal amounts of water and sunshine. Several times a day a member of the group would concentrate his power of thought on one seed and declare that it would die. Then he concentrated his Power on the other seed and declared that it would grow and flourish. The one seed died and the other flourished into a thriving plant. In one instance the Power was used to restrict the Power expressing as the seed and the Power as that seed shriveled and departed.

The results are the same in the human body and human affairs. If you use your Power to find fault with your body and your circumstances, you are using the Power to restrict the Power. In the same way the Power responds to praise, gratitude and delight. This is its nature and purpose.

Every thought, belief and result is the action and reaction of the one Power upon its own self. It is the means by which Life makes demands upon itself for new expressions of itself, and responds to those demands from within itself.

Now that we have prepared our minds to accept the truth that we are Life using Power, the next step is *how* to apply it in our every day life. For after all, our world and our dominion over it, is composed of the experiences of our every day life, and our dominion over them.

HEALTH IS YOUR NATURAL STATE

Before we can intelligently deal with experience we must divide experience into its natural categories.

Every experience that man can have falls into one of these four general categories–Health, Supply, Happiness and Self-Expression.

Every experience that we would want changed is one in which the Power is not being expressed in one of these categories. For instance, the experience of sickness is the absence of the expression of the Power as Health. The experience of poverty is the absence of the expression of the Power as Supply. The experience of unhappiness is the absence of the Power as Love in one of its forms. The experience of frustration is the absence of the expression of the Power as Self-Expression.

Before there can be a boy absent from school there must be a boy. All experiences of a negative nature, which result from the absence of our positive use of the Power, can be changed to their opposite by the presence of the Power's positive use. And within us is the ability to change this absence to a presence. Let us take an example in each of the four categories.

Suppose you are sick. Regardless of what form this sickness takes it is the absence of Health. It is the result of an unnatural state. Health is our *Natural State*, else we would never recover from our first illness. Thus we see that Health is one of the forms taken by this Power which accomplishes all of Life's purposes.

Therefore, to remove the illness simply means to enable the Power as Health to express in our lives where it has not been expressing. This is what we must cause to happen. But, how are we to do it?

Let us turn back in our thought to what we learned was the way in which the Power is activated. In the story of the Zen Buddhist monk and throughout the Bible we are told that to activate the Power all *we* have to do is to delight in its existence. So, that is what we must do, *delight in its existence.* The reason why it has escaped us before is because we must delight in Power right in the *midst* of the pain, just as the monk *returned* the burden to his back before he began to make a joyful noise unto the Power.

We can have many diseases, but all have the same cure, which is to enable the Power as Health to express itself where hitherto it has been restricted.

The first step is to use our authority to direct our attention. Where shall our attention be directed first? To the fact that we are alive. We will accept that we are alive. Now then, let us turn our attention to the denial of our illness as belonging to this Life that is us. It is very important to understand that we deny a thing, not because it is, but because it is not. True denial is to see there is nothing in Reality to deny. Our Natural State of Health, which is the

Reality of our being, contains no illness to deny. How long does it take to dispose of that which is not real?

We must have the courage to deny appearances when they deny our Natural State. We must acknowledge that at all times we have the Power of dominion and that we must use this Power to establish our Natural State in *all* our ways – not just a few ways.

There is one aspect of the Power which, when we think on it, can always cause us to delight in it. It is this – DELIGHT DOETH THE WORK. To delight in it is *all* the Power is *waiting* for to sweep through into manifestation. This is its nature – to respond to recognition and delight.

We do not have to struggle. We do not have to fight. We only need to know and when we know, we cannot help but feel a sense of joy and praise and gratitude.

Is it not delightful that all we have to do to remove the absence of Health, is to delight in Health as our Natural State?

When we understand this our spirits naturally soar – no matter how sick we are at the moment. Of course this state of delight is not accomplished all at once. The sicker we are the more difficult it is to have control of our attention, the more difficult it is to turn our attention away from our pain, limitation and despair. But, we *can make a start* and we *can* accomplish the state of optimism and cheerfulness even if we can't at first feel that first surge of delight.

A state of cheerfulness as a result of this knowledge is all that is needed to release the Power as Health to and through the very point and the very place where it has been restricted.

Isn't it wonderful to know that to be cheerful is all that is required of us to remove that which causes us not to be cheerful? Is not this something to be cheerful about?

So, to heal ourselves, let us remember that what our thoughts refuse to accept, our body cannot continue to express. For, as we know, the body is not self-acting but is acted upon by the Power channeled through our thoughts. Since our attention directs Power, we can say, *Attention is Power.*

The truth to remember about healing is this, "If you are not cheerful, you are not creative!" To be cheerful about these truths releases the creative Power which causes our Natural State of Health to be our experience. Thus we can see that DELIGHT DOETH THE WORK.

In doing the work, the Power has the power to use US to accomplish ITS purposes. For instance, it has the power to CHANGE our attitudes if they are causing us not to observe the natural laws of Health.

And the Power does it in such a WAY that we PREFER to do what is best for our Health. We find that we prefer different foods and food combinations, and our habits of sleep and exercise begin to change. Not with a feeling of privation and drudgery, but as a new and thrilling adventure.

In all four categories of experience, the Power has the power, to cause *us* to cooperate with it in its purpose of removing restrictions to the expression of our inherent potentials, IF we are the RESTRICTOR. And the delightful part is that the Power has WAYS of making our cooperation with it the most delightful thing we COULD do. For, THIS is the way nature causes us to do everything we do.

Therefore, if we will prime the pump, by delighting in the power, IT will do the rest... IT will do the WORK.

CREATIVE CAPSULE FOR HEALTH

"Because I am alive I am already one with Life's Powers and Purposes. Life's Natural State is Health. I now delight in this truth, knowing that, as I do, I activate the Power and it removes all that has prohibited my Health from being my experience."

"That which "causes" my delight is the truth that all I have to do to remove the absence of Health is to delight in Health as my Natural State. And, each new evidence of my increasing Health naturally increases my delight."

"It is so delightful that delight doeth the work - and the work increaseth the delight."

*After reading the above affirmative thought, enter into the Silence and jot down any images and/or feelings that arise in a journal. Remember Spirit is doing the work in you, as you. That is Delightful!

SUPPLY IS YOUR NATURAL STATE

Now then, let us consider the second category, Supply.

Let us turn our attention to Life, the Life that we are, and ask ourselves the question – Could there be Life and also that which Life needs to express itself? Could our Deity give us the gift of Life without *including* in the gift that which is *necessary* to accept the gift, to enjoy the gift? Therefore, Life must contain within *itself* the means to fulfill and enjoy itself.

There could not be Life *and* that which Life needs. There must be Life *as* what Life needs. But how does it work?

It naturally works within that which is natural to us, else it couldn't work at all. In answer to the question of man's needs Jesus told his followers to, "Take a look at the way it worked in other forms of Life. For instance, consider the lilies of the field. They do not have to go outside their own nature or their natural environment to receive all that is needed for their full expression."

In the same way, the Creator knows what we have need of and has *included* Life's needs within the very nature of Life itself.

Jesus said "Seek first the Kingdom of God and all things you need will be added."

What is the Kingdom of God and where and how are we to seek it? What do we seek with and where can it be found?

It has to be where everyone can find it, else there would be discrimination. Everyone has to have the same chance of seeking and finding. And everyone does have this equal chance. That is what is meant by everyone being created equal.

That which we seek *with* is our life – our own awareness, our own knowledge and acceptance. And that which we seek *for* is the Kingdom of God – which means the knowledge and acceptance of the Authority of Good.

The Kingdom of God means the absolute authority of our own Good. This is the only Reality – our Natural State is to have all the Good we *need* for a full and happy life.

So, just as in the first category of Health, we find that Supply is also our Natural State, and any experience to the contrary is just where the Power as Supply is absent of not being expressed.

How do we know when we have fulfilled our part and have found the Kingdom? We know by our feelings. Do we still feel the same way or do we have a sense of joy and delight? We have to believe that we have already received our Good within our own Nature, because this is the way nature has provided that we experience it. If we believe this, we can not possibly feel the same way as when we do not believe it.

The natural way by which we bring into our lives our Good is to believe that we have already received it as a natural part of Life itself. So, once again, we find that the Discipline of Delight is the means to the attainment of our Good. And, once again, just as in the midst of pain, also in the midst of limitation, we must turn our attention upon the truth that our needed Good is our Natural State and to delight in this truth activates the Power whose purpose it is to bring the needed Good into our life. Thus again – Delight Doeth the Work.

To be creative really does not mean that we create anything that has not already been created. It simply means that we allow the purposes of creation to fulfill themselves in our lives. So, if we are cheerful about this truth, then we are being creative, because we are fulfilling the part we are to play in enabling our Good to come through.

If we cannot accept this truth, if we have been unable to find a place within our belief for the Kingdom of Good, then we are still holding back its expression in our life and we will continue to experience the absence of our Good to which we have given the names of poverty and limitation.

Thus we see that success is not on the outside, but is the inside coming out. Our dominion is not over the outside world, but over the inside world of our own beliefs and reactions. And, our inside world has dominion over the outside world.

Is this not delightful? Is this not something to be cheerful about? Can we not be cheerfully creative right in the midst of our limitation when we know that our very cheerfulness opens wide the door through which the Power flows, bringing with it our individually needed Good?

The reason cheerfulness is emphasized is because it is a state of consciousness which we can know when we have and when we do not have. Such a state as faith is so indefinite that we are never quite sure when we have it and when we do not. But, we do know when we are cheerful and when we are not. And, with the simplified truths contained herein, we can, at will, deliberately become cheerful, thereby, deliberately opening our Life to the flow of the Good which is our Natural State.

If we still feel the same way about our prospects, then we do not believe in Good as our Natural State and we cannot be cheerful about it. But, if we believe that our Good is already following us, then we can be and are cheerful. Therefore, cheerfulness is the measure of our belief, the measure of our creativity.

Isn't it wonderful? What if we had to be sad in order to be creative? The nature of Life is so beautifully and exquisitely simple that it confounds us. It is simply this – Since the purpose of Life is every expanding joy, in order to activate the Power, we must conform to the purpose of Life and enter into some degree of joy. Otherwise, it would be possible to use the Power to defeat the purpose for which it was designed to serve.

In a word, we can't be joyful if we are sad and since to be joyful is the purpose which the Power serves, it can only be activated through joy.

So once again, the Discipline of Delight is the

answer, the answer to our needed supply. We delight that Supply is our Natural State and DELIGHT DOETH THE WORK.

CREATIVE CAPSULE FOR SUPPLY

"Because I am alive, that which my life needs in order to fulfill its purpose is included within the very nature of life itself. My Ample Supply is my Natural State because, from the beginning, the Creative Intelligence knew I would have need of these things.

"I now use the Power to release my supply by delighting in the truth that Ample Supply is my Natural State. Ample Supply means being able to do what I want to do when I want to do it. All the riches in the world could give me no more because that is all I could need.

"That which causes my delight is the truth, that all I have to do to remove that which separates me from my needs is delight in Ample Supply as my Natural State. My delight activates the Power whose Purpose it is to provide me with all my needs.

"As my supply increases, my delight will increase which, in turn, will increase the Power. It is so delightful that delight doeth the work and the work increaseth the delight."

*After reading the above affirmative thought, enter into the Silence and jot down any images and/or feelings that arise in a journal. Remember Spirit is doing the work in you, as you. That is Delightful!

HAPPINESS IS YOUR NATURAL STATE

Let us now turn our attention to the third category which is Happiness. The first thing we must understand about Happiness is that it is not a cause, but an effect. We cannot take Happiness by storm, for Happiness is a by-product of Life fulfilling itself.

Happiness is the reward of cooperating with Life's purpose. The thought that we must sustain throughout our consideration of this third category is this – Happiness is not a station along Life's highway, but a manner of traveling.

In order to creatively approach this third category of human experience, we again must reduce it to its common denominator. We must relate it to life's overall purpose and running through these categories is the thread of the truth that the purpose of Life is ever-expanding joy.

This following statement will give us a key by which we can bring Happiness into any situation. The statement is this – Happiness is the *result* of *mixing* love with life. All unhappiness is the result of the *absence* of love in some form – the absence of the love of God, love of man, or love of self.

The attainment in awareness which will enable us to overcome all absences of love which we call unhappiness is this: everyone is the incarnation of Love and the purpose of all experience is to discover it. If God is Love, then His Creation is also Love.

Our greatest difficulty comes because we do not understand the truth that there are two currents involved in love. One is being loved and the other is doing the loving. When we are first born and until we are grown, we need to be loved and nature has provided that we are loved. But, once we are grown our need changes. Our need then is to love and all of man's difficulty comes from his lack of understanding of this truth, for he is still trying to be loved when the fulfillment of all his Good depends upon him loving. Not only the fulfillment of his inner Good or Happiness, but the fulfillment of his outside good, is reflected in his circumstances.

To love fulfills the law of our Happiness as well as the law of our harmonious circumstance. To love fulfills the purpose of Life and the proof of that fulfillment is joy. To be loved is something that happens to someone else, for someone else is doing the loving. Only if you love is anything happening to you and only as something different happens to you, can something different come into your life.

But, we ask ourselves, how can we love those who are not loving in their actions? We can love them if we understand that their true nature is the incarnation of Love, and that every unlovely and unloving expression comes from their seeking to be loved instead of seeking to love. No one is ever guilty of anything but this misunderstanding.

Everyone senses that love is the center of Life's orbit. That is why we approach every situation with either love or the withholding of love.

No one can keep you from loving him. And if we look to the true person, which is the personification of undiscovered love, we will always find something that is very, very worthy of and inspiring of our love.

Thus, as in our previous categories, once again, we find that love is our Natural State and that all unhappiness is the result of our Natural State having been restricted in its expression.

To know that love is our true nature and that love is every other person's true nature and that the purpose of our experience is to discover this, is one of the most delightful of truths. And, to delight in this truth opens wide the doors of our heart and enables the Power to sweep through, removing all that has hitherto blinded our eyes.

The Discipline of Delight once again provides us with the "open sesame" of this glorious aspect. It is this which brings vitality, color and beauty to life. Love is what makes joy joyous.

So, wherever there is unhappiness you can know that it is nature telling us that, at this point, we have restricted love. There is someone or something or someplace from which we are restricting our love, and the point of points to remember in our attitude toward our ability to love is this – we are not dealing with *our* love, we are dealing with an attribute of God *shared* with us. There is not my love and your love. There is only one love – the Love of God. It is a functional part of our nature and we can love just as freely, just as deliberately, as we can feel or hear or speak or move.

So, let us not deceive ourselves into thinking that there is a person or a situation we cannot love. There are only people and situations which we refuse to love.

Thus we find that the most delightful part of Happiness is that we can have it at will. Why is this true? Because not only is our Natural State the incarnation of Love, but also, our Natural State is the ability to love at will. And to love at will enables us to be happy at will. To delight in this wondrous truth which is our Natural State will bring new and unsuspected opportunities of Happiness and Love.

We are created by Love, in Love, out of Love, and for Love. This is our Natural State and to delight in it enables the Power to release the flow of love wherever it is needed to bring Happiness.

Thus again – DELIGHT DOETH THE WORK.

CREATIVE CAPSULE FOR HAPPINESS

"Because I am alive, I am an individualization of Love. Happiness is the reward of discovering my own love nature. Unhappiness is the way life tells me that I am restricting my love from God, my fellow man or myself. I know that my need is to love and not to be loved, for to love fulfills all the laws of my good.

"I know that Love is my Natural State and the Natural State of everyone else. To delight in this truth activates the Power which reveals to me my love nature and reveals to those I love their love nature.

"That which causes my delight is the wonderful truth that all I have to do to make new discoveries of my love nature is to delight in Love as my Natural State.

"My delight activates the Power and the Power increasingly reveals that which is lovable and loving in all that comes into my life. And since love blended with life is happiness, my happiness increases with my love. It is so delightful that delight doeth the work and the work increaseth the delight."

*After reading the above affirmative thought, enter into the Silence and jot down any images and/or feelings that arise in a journal. Remember Spirit is doing the work in you, as you. That is Delightful!

CREATIVE SELF-EXPRESSION IS YOUR NATURAL STATE

In the fourth category, as in the other three, we find of necessity that we are dealing with a faculty which is natural to us.

Creative Self-Expression has to be an inherent potential, else we could never bring it forth. We do not plant our potentials, we already have received them. This is what Jesus referenced to when he told us to believe we had already received. And we can believe we have already received potentials. To have a potential is one thing – to express that potential is something quite different.

An acorn is one thing, an oak tree something else. However, one is dependent on, and is an expression of, the other. That which is potential, or universal, remains, but a Universal Potential until it is individualized. However, without the Universal to draw from there could be no individualization. Thus, we see that the Universal NEEDS the individual and individual of itself is helpless without the Universal from which to express Itself.

All three previous categories are prerequisites to the expression of Life itself. In order to express, life must be physically fit. This is the health department.

In addition to the physical instrument being capable, it must have its material needs met in order to move here and there under conditions that are favorable. This we call Supply.

The first two categories, health and supply, deal with the instrument of experience and *its* needs. The second two deal with "Purpose' of the instrument, which is the unfoldment and development of the one who is having the experience.

The third category, happiness, deals with the emotional health of the consciousness which is using the instrument. And the fourth category, self-expression, deals with the reason for the first three – which is the unfoldment of the Eternal Life inhabiting and using the physical instrument of experience.

"Know ye not that ye are the temple of the Holy Spirit?"

It is not the temple and its needs, but the Spirit and its needs that we are dealing with in the third and fourth categories.

But, once again, in the fourth category, we are not left alone but are directed by the Power that serves all of Deity's purposes.

The direction we receive as to the unfoldment of the Eternal Spirit, which employs the instrument of experience, is in the form we call desire. What is desire? What must it be? It is a voice that comes to us from within ourselves. What else could it be except the voice of our Potential seeking to express itself in a way that only our particular growing edge, our particular point and place of development could provide.

Let us take a look at the word desire. The very word means "from" or "of the Father." Sire means "father." Thus, that which we feel as a desire is the father aspect of the Power seeking to father a new expression of itself through us. This is why we should never attempt to be anything other than that which we feel compelled to be. Everyone has a special kind of genius. In all of nature there are no two things alike. Not even two blades of grass are the same. To respond to the Power as it tries to express through us as our desire, is the way we fulfill our own particular genius.

But, we say to ourselves – I work in a shop; I work in an office; I am a housewife; I am a salesman; how can I be different or a genius? No matter how conforming and monotonous our activities seem to be, everyone does them a little differently and makes a different contribution. If we want to excel or if we want to be removed from where we are, the way to do it is to respond to our own desires.

Do whatever you are doing the way that you want to do it, for it isn't *you* that is wanting it that way, in an arbitrary attitude, but it is the Power, by which Life makes new demands upon itself for new expressions of itself, seeking to use you as the means of this fulfillment.

Accept your desire and act upon it. It is true that you may misinterpret what the desire basically is, and your actions might be imprudent in the opinion of the general public, but the worse thing that can result is that you have misinterpreted Life's call upon you for your cooperation. Even this misinterpretation is more valuable, more progressive, than if you had turned deaf ears and compelled yourself to remain in a frustrated circumstance and state of consciousness.

Our desires are the way the Power tells us what's *next* in our unfoldment. Unfoldment of what? Unfoldment of our own creativity.

In the fourth category we are dealing with the unfoldment of our divine Sonship. We are created in the image of God's creativity. We are an incarnation of the creative process. Why? Because we are Gods in the making. Each of us is a God seed. Each of us has as our destiny the creating and governing of a world of our own.

We are discovering our creativity now in this theatre of operation. This is why we were given dominion over its laws and Powers. This is why the fourth category is the most important. It is the one in which we further the *purpose* of our life from an *eternal* standpoint and is why nature gives us the sense of frustration if we are not experiencing creative self-expression.

Where would the logical place be for our creative self-expression?

If it is to serve our over-all growth from an eternal standpoint, it must be at the exact point of our growing edge – Our growing edge being the sum total of all that we have expressed creatively up to now.

The next point of growth in a plant is from where it has already grown and all that has gone before which supports its new growth. This is why everyone's desire for creative self-expression is different and why we should never turn deaf ears to the voice of the next step in our unfolding Godhood.

This desire, this voice of Power, does not always speak to us in terms of the need for an artistic attainment, by which we mean the expression of music, literature, etc., because our next growth, our next need, might very well be in the realm of qualities of consciousness itself.

It is just as creative to be able to express a greater quality of kindness or understanding as to paint a picture, and quite often, the inability to express such a quality is the bottleneck which prohibits us from extending our growing edge.

Now the wonderful part of this fourth category is in the subtle operation of the Power. We can understand it in a measure when we remember that all things work together to accomplish the purpose of Life, and when we deliberately cooperate with the purpose, we enable all things to automatically work for our good.

To cooperate with the fourth category causes the first three to automatically fulfill themselves because the first three are designed to make the fourth one possible - possible and pleasant. The absence of health, the absence of supply, the absence of happiness is quite frequently the result of absence of creative self-expression.

Before we can love, we have to have something to love *with*. We have to have self-esteem and feel on center with ourselves; else, we are not loving but seeking love in an effort to provide us with the self-esteem and sense of being on center which is lacking. So, the most important category in our life is our creative self-expression for it is where the past and the future are focused in the here and now.

But, we say to ourselves, how can I be creative in my hum-drum mediocre circumstances? The reason our circumstances seem hum-drum and mediocre is because we have refused to respond to the voice of our desire. Our creativity need not be some sweeping enactment. It can be but the alteration of an attitude. This effort on our part opens the door and enables the Power to come through and cause all things to work together for our good. The Power has ways we know not of, and compensations we know not of. So, let us not attempt to measure what the Power can do in a creative way in the fulfillment of our desire.

For once again, we find we are dealing with our Natural State and the Power which serves it. Our Natural State is a God-seed and the only way we can discover our Godhood is by the use of our God-Power and of Creative Self-Expression.

To know that every experience has a value which far excels that of which the experience is composed is a truth which, when we know, provides us with the delight of delights. That value which is so delightful is this - regardless of what an experience is, in its truest significance, it is but our Godhood using, seeking, and finding itself. Is this not something to be cheerful about? Can we not, under any circumstance, delight in the truth of our own deity?

We hear the voice of our own deity speaking to us as our desire. The desire is the *next* creativeness we are to discover as our own. To delight in our desires, as the directing voice of our awakening Godhood, is the *way* we activate the Power of our own creative self-expression. Thus once again - DELIGHT DOETH THE WORK.

CREATIVE CAPSULE FOR SELF-EXPRESSION

"Because I am alive, I am a God-seed whose destiny is ever-increasing Creative Self-Expression. I am an individualization of the Creative Process and the purpose of my experience is to discover my own Creativity.

"My Creative Potential speaks to me in the voice of desire. My desire is what it is because it is the way the Power pin-points what is 'NEXT' in the process of my self-discovery.

"To delight in my desire as the directing voice of my own awakening Godhood activates the Power which causes the whispering potential to become a reality. The Power provides me with the correct interpretation of my desire and the necessary enthusiasm and capacity to bring it forth as my creative self-expression. The fulfillment of one desire opens the door for the next. So, even as the spiral grows I leave the old home for the new. Thus, to delight in Creative Self-Expression as my Natural State causes my potentials to express themselves in ever increasing ways.

"It is so delightful that delight doeth the work and the work increaseth the delight."

*After reading the above affirmative thought, enter into the Silence and jot down any images and/or feelings that arise in a journal. Remember Spirit is doing the work in you, as you. That is Delightful!

YOU ARE YOUR POWER

Let us now provide for ourselves a place to which we can turn for a simple formula, with which we can, at will, both fulfill the needs of our instrument, and progress toward the purpose of the eternal life that is using the instrument.

Then, we will not only have multiplied the nation, but we will be increasing the joy. This in no way leaves out God, but as Jesus said, "Herein is our Father glorified when we use our Father-given Power to accomplish our Father-given Purpose."

No longer will *we* cry - "How can we reach God?" For, now we know we do not have to reach God but that, because of the very obvious fact that we are alive, we are already one with Him; that God is our "Callable Good," and within the *natural functions* of our life is the means by which we call the Good into our experience.

Suppose we want to call forth Health. How do we do it?

First we turn our attention to the fact that we are alive. This causes us to accept the truth that we are already one with all that is natural to life.

Then we move our acceptance to the truth that Health is Life's Natural State. Next, we remember that there is a Power whose purpose is to remove everything contrary to Life's Natural states, and this Power is activated by our delight in its existence and purpose.

As we delight in the Power we realize that even

though there are many so-called diseases, they all have the *same* cure. And what is that? It is Health - our Natural State!

Let us provide for ourselves a "Creative Capsule," that we can "swallow" into our acceptance which will automatically heal us from any of Life's needs. Since there are but four basic needs, we will require but four capsules.

The affirmations that follow each of the chapters on the four Natural States will provide and assist in healing any of Life's needs.

OUR MANNER OF TRAVELING

So, we have found that the *art of living* is reduced to the *art of deliberate delight*. And we master this art as we habitually remind ourselves that we are alive, and because we are, we are also the Power with which we can make our life what we desire. This will enable us to make, "loving self-expression" our, "manner of traveling" and then happiness will go with us every step of the way.

It is natural that our first step along the *HIGH*way of self-discovery is a difficult one, for it is the one in which we have to accept *completely* that our *real* world is a *mental* world.

Why is this the first step? Because, before we can control the thought that controls the circumstance, we must become *aware* of the thought. We must become as *aware* of our states of mind as we are of our body, and must become as *capable* of directing and changing our thoughts as we are of moving our body from one room to another.

How can we become habitually *aware* of our thoughts? How can we change them to what they need to be to change our circumstances? First, let us realize that "An ounce of prevention is worth a pound of cure" is more true on the mental plane that anywhere else. It is far better to prevent a negative state of mind than to attempt to cure it after it has "taken us over." Once we are in it, we are thinking *with* it and *from* it, and it is very difficult to change our thoughts when we have to use the thoughts we are thinking to do the changing.

Therefore, it would be exceedingly valuable to us to auto-condition ourselves in such a way that the *very experiences* through which we move each day would serve to remind us of the nature of experience. To the extent that we do this automatically as we enter into each experience and identify it with the category to which it belongs, it will cause that category of experience to *activate* in our lives in its Natural State, instead of its unnatural state.

For instance, when we get up in the morning we should condition ourselves in such a way that the very act of arising will cause us to pause and raise our consciousness. The aim is to get to the point where we automatically think on the wondrous gift of Life itself, the gift of the new day, with its opportunity for a fuller and richer experience of the four categories through which Life expresses itself.

As we eat breakfast we should let this daily activity remind us of the category of Health, that Health is our Natural State. To remember it causes us to delight in it, and to delight in it causes Health to express in an increased way. Our breakfast will be more delicious and its benefits to us will be greatly increased. This keeps us from letting a negative state get started. It is not only the ounce of prevention but also the activation of new glory in our life.

As we go to work or go into the activities of the

day which provide us with our material needs, we should condition ourselves to cause our work to remind us that Ample Supply is our Natural State, and when we remind ourselves of this truth it causes us to delight in its truth. This results in our work becoming increasingly more valuable to all concerned.

As we come into contact with other people we should condition ourselves in such a way that every time another person comes into our presence, every time we have occasion to converse with another, we should let that remind us that every person's Natural State and our Natural State is the embodiment of Love. The *purpose* of the contact is to *help* each other *discover* it. This will automatically cause us to express Love, and that will automatically bring forth the expression of love in a new way from the other person. This habitual attitude toward others, set in motion by the very act of contact with them, will provide ever-increasing overtones of happiness and friendliness to every human relationship.

In our daily activity, every time our thoughts turn to our own personal self-expression, whether it is in the form of a needed decision, no matter how small, or the feeling of frustration, we should so condition ourselves that in either case a bell would ring - so to speak - and our thoughts would automatically be moved to remembrance of the truth that Creative Self-Expression is our Natural State. As we think on it and delight in it, we know that the Power will give us the right decision. If we are still in a state of frustration, the Power will be activated to show us the way and provide us with the necessary enthusiasm and know-how.

In this way, we use the four categories of experience to automatically direct our thoughts in such a way that will cause us to *automatically increase* the Natural expression of those categories in our life. This is the way we become the *habitual director* of *our own creativity*.

The wonderful part of our dominion over our mental world is that we are never dealing with anything except the thought of the moment.

The only thought that ever needs healing is the thought of the moment and that one we *can* change.

This truth gave rise to the statement, "Life by the yard is hard but by the inch is a cinch."

There are only present thoughts. Thoughts of the past are still present thoughts - just as thoughts of the future are present thoughts. Thus we can say that the only thing that ever needs to be healed is the present thought, for if we heal *IT, IT* will heal the circumstance.

We must have the courage to change our thoughts about appearances. Lives are changed as thoughts are rearranged, and a changed feeling always comes with a changed thought.

If appearances deny the truth of our dominion over our world as our Natural State, then we must have the courage to deny the appearances as being anything except an absence of the expression of our Natural State. And our denial must be accompanied by a feeling of delight else we do not believe our denial.

We must delight in Health as our Natural State even in the midst of pain. We must delight in Ample Supply as our Natural State even in the midst of lack. We must delight in Happiness as our Natural State even in the midst of despair. We must delight in Creative Self-Expression as our Natural State even in the midst of frustration. *This* makes the change!

Since the Power is activated by delight, it follows that the Discipline of Delight is the "open sesame" of Human Destiny.

For delight doeth the work and the work increaseth the delight, and the delight increaseth the work, from glory to glory, worlds without end!

EPILOGUE

"There is no real desire without the potential ability to fulfill it, and there is no latent ability without the opportunity to call it into expression" says Emmet Fox[2]. Dr. Mike would concur. What I know is this: our aspirations create our inspirations. Therefore, if we fail to act on our inspirations, we fail to honor God, who is a Universal Presence that lives in us, as us.

Some believe in predestination in one form or another. Science today believes in genetics which is one of the many forms that lend credence to pre-destination. For example, our genetic codes determine the color of our eyes, skin, hair, bone structure and so on. Of course the question is "What determined or made the codes? Who created the genesis of genetics or better yet, the orderliness of the Universe?"

For me the answer is this: There is only One Mind, and each of us is the individualization of this Mind. Our authentic self knows that we conspire with God to express values which resemble our Godlikeness. Anything less than that is a *mis*creation, a mistake, something created for our learning. The Spirit within us, as us, gives birth to the form that we identify with ourselves; it even delivers us into a certain culture that has entrenched

[2] Fox, Emmet. 1993 *Diagrams For Living*, San Francisco, California, HarperSanFrancisco, 229 pages, FirstHarperCollins paperback edition.

beliefs. If this feels like or seem like predestination, where does free choice come into play? How can we change our circumstances?

We all have witnessed change for the better in others and hopefully within ourselves. We sense or know there is a rhythm, a balance and an order to all that we observe. There is something greater than we are of which we are a part that allows us the freedom to make choices. We are not freed from the consequence of our choices. That is where we learn from experience, is it not? As scientists, as students of truth, as individuals, we sense we are all here for a purpose. We appreciate being a part of life, a part of nature.

The ancient scientists realized a rhythm, an order to the planets and stars and determined we are linked to them. Twelve signs of the Zodiac in ancient days were understood to influence the lives of everyone born under a different sign, in a particular moment. Astrological scientists put as much credence in what they discovered as do genetic scientists today. Astrology is no more or less an art than any other science. The real value comes from understanding what it means.

In the art of Astrology, certain characteristics, traits, and faculties seem to be imbued in us that relate to the Zodiac. It is no accident that there are twelve signs of the Zodiac, twelve months of the year, twelve disciples of Lord Jesus, or twelve leaders of the tribes of Israel. The value in a sign is what we give to it, what it means. Regarding the twelve leaders of the tribes of Israel, what they mean to a Spiritual Psychologist like Emmet Fox is: "They stand for the foundation faculties of the human soul, and the lesson here is that unless all our faculties are oriented toward one point, we are not going to conquer the heathen (unenlightened way of being) within ourselves."[3] So it always comes back to: **How do we lighten up?**

In biblical terms, we are here to get understanding. True understanding brings light into our consciousness. That is called elucidation or lightening up. Elucidation is an express of delight. (of the Light, in the Light, as the Light). You know the one we hide under a bushel basket. How many of us remember what a bushel basket is? I'd like to remember how to spell it!

Delight transfers our egotistically based fears. Fears that often result in the flight or fight syndrome are transformed into being here now. When we are totally present, we are in the Presence and that is a delight. In the Presence we experience Peace, Unconditional Love. This is expressing our authentic self.

We do not slay or conquer our egos as in a battle; rather we pay attention to our feelings and thoughts and see if they seem to be restricting or diminutive. If they are, we can change them. That is where we use the power to change. No matter what

---

[3] Fox, Emmet. 1993 *Diagrams For Living*, San Francisco, California, HarperSanFrancisco, 229 pages, FirstHarperCollins paperback edition.

sign we are born under, no matter what our human characteristics or traits are, no matter what our DNA produces in our complex human structure, we can change for the better. As we know, there is a Power that does restore, make new, heal, resolve and dissolve problems. Arnold Michael gave us guidance on how the power works as we work with it.

1. You can <u>return to the four creative capsules chapters</u> regarding our Health, Supply, Happiness and Self-Expression. Re-read them and use them to build spiritual muscles, so to speak. This is not an instant fix; it takes work and discipline in any field to achieve the desired results

2. <u>Refer to your journal</u> that you kept from your Silent meditations. This is how you increase your awareness of how Spirit is working in you, as you.

3. <u>Refer to the Astrological Chart in the Appendix</u> of this book. Determine what strengths, what gifts, you may have brought into this expression of life, as well as what you may need to work on to remove any restrictions to your authentic self. Remember the signs are only indications or tendencies.

The Golden Key is finding in prayer, in meditation, in the Silent Discipline of Delight your Essential Divinity.

In our god*less*ness, when we miss the mark of being perfected in the spirit, the painfulness of separation seems to have dominion. In God*ful*ness, separation is obsolete. Our authentic self has real dominion. In the practice of the Silent Discipline of Delight we come to know and realize that Life expresses Itself through us, through our desires. "De" "Sire". All pure desire is the will of God; "de" meaning of, "sire" meaning Father, will or ego. We all have ego and spirit.

Ego is will and Spirit is willing for us to discover our authentic selves and to use our gifts to help each other reach our full potential. Doing the work is a labor of Love, and Joy takes the labor out of it. Oh! Happy days are here again when our spirit and our ego work in harmony with Ego/Spirit.

Cheers,

Charlie Sommer

THE MADONNA MINISTRY

The Madonna Ministry Hold These Truths To Be Self-evident*
By Charles Sommer

Everyone has their understanding of what "Truth" is: All of us interpret through our own filters what we hold to be self-evident. Dr. Arnold Michael, the founder of this ministry, and I attended the same college where we were trained as ministers and teachers. We had many of the same spiritual interests and understandings. What we understand may change tomorrow, what is "Truth" will never change.

We hold these truths to be Self-evident: God is Spirit and Spirit resides everywhere. Spirit is Omni active Love/Intelligence. There is One Mind, One Life and One Presence. To know God can only be discerned spiritually. The fruits of Spirit are Love, Joy, Peace and Assurance. These are the fruits of the Spiritual Kingdom. As spiritual beings, each of us has the free choice to express spiritual qualities of the kingdom. We are free to choose but not free from the consequences of our choices. The Laws of Karma, Cause and Effect, and Recompense act as our teacher and always response in kind.

The ultimate fulfillment of the Law is to express the resemblance of God. We understand that God is Love-Light-Power. To know God is to Love God first and then thy neighbor as thy self. There is no gift greater than

Love and Joy. Peace and Blessed Assurance are emanations of It.

How does the Absolute Work through us as us? As viewed from the Spiritual Trinity here is how it works: The Divine Father Principle is the Word of God and the Divine Mother Principle is the Expression of God. To know God is to Express God's immaculate words. The Divine Mother within us all receives the direct impressions of the all-pervasive Divine Father. The inspirational ideas conceived at the Godhead impregnate the Divine Mother who, as the Creative Medium, gives birth to all creation. The creation of the Absolute, First Cause, the Great I Am, is holy, completely acceptable unto the Law of Being. This is the quintessence of creative expression. This is the Trinity of Being.

Who are we? We are individualization of God. As god/goddess, our task, if we choose it, is to minister Love into expression. To the extent we do this we are fulfilling the Law of our being. We recognize that we are spiritual beings seeking the resemblance of God's unadulterated expression. To the extent that we express the fruits of the kingdom of God we are ministering Love-Light-Power. We each bring gifts of the Spirit into each incarnation. Some have the gift of prophecy, intellect, language, clairvoyance, clairaudience, and healing, Yet it is Love that is the common denominator and numerator of Life Itself. To honor God within the temple of our spiritual being is to express our Godlikeness. We express our creativity in particular ways that are congruent with and resonate with the Wholeness or Holiness of our essential nature, which is divine. "There is no sin, but a mistake, and no punishment, but a consequence."

How do we learn? We gods/goddess can learn from our mis-creations, which invite pain and suffering into our experience. We have an eternity to get it right. We can also learn from an inner awareness that goes beyond the veil of separation to elucidation. The illusion of what seems to be is surrendered. The spiritual discernment of what truly *Is* becomes known. Unity is the unadulterated truth in It's multiplicity of expression. Visibility, invisibility and divisibility are perceptions that attempt to explain the full spectrum of understanding, from what is called the gross material to enlightened understanding. Elucidation is enlightened understanding.

What are we here to express? Our task is not to find fault. It is not to hold grievances. It is to seek the kingdom of God within ourselves and express it wholly (holy) and completely. It is not God that makes us suffer. It is our misuse of the creative process. Call it karmic justice or ignorance. Of what are we ignorant? We are ignoring our essential nature. It is through the Law of Cause and Effect and through many incarnations that we have learned to respect the Law and to choose what God wills. We understand that God's will is first to Love God and to Love thy neighbor as thy self. Through prayer, meditation, simple acts of kindness, and sensing the innate beauty in all Nature, we become increasingly aware of the Divine Presence within our body temples. Through genuine gratitude and true humility God expresses the quintessence of Itself through us as us. We have become the chosen ones because we have chosen to express what God truly is. In meekness we accept our anointment by Spirit and willingly return good for evil. Complete forgiveness opens the portal to effectively practice non-resistance, and non violence. Love is the self-giving-ness of Spirit expressing Itself through creation. Creativity Mind is the Feminine Principle of Universal Life. We are creative beings. We are here to express our creativity in beneficial ways.

What does it mean to minister? We are here to minister Love-Light-Power in bringing the Divine Ideas into expression. The Divine Ideas are perfect images held forever in the Mind of God. For example: The Divine Man or Woman resides as the immaculate Concept in the Mind of God. As we turn our attention to what God really is, Love, we enable ourselves to be aligned with the Mind of God. In this awareness we practice the presence of God and our consciousness opens to the Divine Influx. The Etheric Vitality pours Itself through the Divine Pattern or the human idea expressed in the true image and likeness of God. Some call the Etheric Vitality the Holy Spirit. It is the Holy Spirit that does restoration, and grants renewal of our mental, emotional and physical bodies. To heal means to make whole. We come into right relationship with the Universe; we are in tune with Infinite. We choose the will to Good and good will is our expression. Fear and limitation give way to realization of what really is and not what appears to be. Intuition is the speech of the Holy Spirit or Holy Comforter. She is often referred to as the third person or principle in the Triune God. We call Her the Holy Madonna, The Holy Mother, The Divine Feminine, The Creative Medium. This is why we call ourselves the Madonna Ministry. We are open to Divine Influx; intuitive knowing guides us into selfless service. There are no walls or barriers to selfless service. The Force is with us. There is no duality in the mind of the minister who knows her self to be ONE

* The Precepts of our Church are fundamental to whatever religious or spiritual persuasion we bring to the Madonna Ministry. They bear repeating:

Basic Precepts of the Madonna Ministry
Precepts are a direction for a rule of action given, we believe, by the Highest Authority:

1. **To love God** (Whatever our understanding of God is!)
2. **To love all humankind as our self**
3. **To express our God-likeness in benevolent service**

We understand that God is love. It makes no difference what name we ascribe to God. What matters is that we realize God's essential nature is love. To know God is to know and express unconditional love. Some ascribe no name to God

To love all humankind is to move beyond the shadows of duality to a realization of unity. In order to do this we must remove the splinter from our own eye (sense of separation). We must be willing to give up our grievances against our brothers and sisters.

To express our God-likeness in beneficial service is the Life Force giving freely of Itself.

HISTORY AND GENERAL INFORMATION

The Madonna Ministry was founded in 1970 by Arnold Michael, D.D., LHD, and his wife Bishop Kathryn Michael. Archbishop Warren Watters was the co-consecrator for Bishop Arnold Michael and later consecrator for both Bishop Kathryn Michael, and Bishop Charles Sommer. Dr. Michael received his Doctorates for his work in Religious Science and for his authorship of "Blessed Among Women" and "Brothers of the Grape."

The Madonna Ministry is rooted on Apostolic Succession historically to the first Christian church founded by Saint Peter and spiritually to all teachers of Truth wherever found. The Madonna Ministry is a sacramental, mystical and Christ-centered church comprised of a voluntary and free association of individuals. We strive to exemplify the highest aspirations of humankind and spirituality, without bias as to race, gender, creed, culture, time, place in history, or manner of reception.

The holy Madonna goes by many names to many cultures: Cosmic Grace, Earth Mother, Holy Comforter, Queen of the Angels, Isis, Quan Yin, Shiva, The Virgin Mary, Our Lady of Guadeloupe, The Immaculate Mother, The Madonna of the Golden Flame, Our Lady of Lourdes, Our Lady of Fatima, Our Lady of Medjugorje, etc.

You may reach the Madonna Ministry website at http://madonnaministry.net.

THE PURPOSE OF THIS INCARNATION

"The heavens declare the glory of God ... day unto day uttereth speech, and night unto night showeth knowledge (energies). There is no speech nor language where their voice is not heard."

Sons of Jacob	Astrological Signs	Motivating Basic Nature	Personality Keynote	Evolutionary Purpose	Helpful Instrument	Has natural tendency of:
GAD	3/22 - 4/31 ARIES	PIONEER	I AM	HUMILITY	MENTAL ENERGY	KINDNESS
JOSEPH	4/21 - 5/21 TAURUS	BUILDER	I HAVE	APPLICATION	COHESION	LOYALTY
BENJAMIN	5/22 - 6/21 GEMINI	INVESTIGATOR	I THINK	CONCENTRATION	ADAPTABILITY	FRIENDLINESS
ISAAC	6/22 - 7/23 CANCER	PATRIOT	I FEEL	SELF-CONFIDENCE	SYMPATHY	LOVE
JUDAH	7/24 - 8/23 LEO	RULER	I WILL	TOLERANCE	FAITH	GENEROSITY
NAPHTALI	8/24 - 9/23 VIRGO	CRITIC	I ANALYZE	DISCRIMINATION	REFLECTION	EXACTNESS
ASHER	9/24 - 10/23 LIBRA	JUDGE	I BALANCE	DECISION	HARMONY	THOUGHTFULNESS
DAN	10/24 - 11/22 SCORPIO	PROBER	I DESIRE	REGENERATION	COURAGE	THOROUGHESS
MANASSEH	11/23 - 12/21 SAGGITARIUS	PHILOSOPHER	I SEE	EXPANSION	GRATITUDE	RIGHTEOUSNESS
ZEBULUN	12/22 - 1/20 CAPRICORN	ORGANIZER	I USE	FORGIVENESS	JUSTICE	COURAGE
REUBEN	1/21 - 2/19 AQUARIUS	HUMANITARIAN	I KNOW	COOPERATION	ALTRUISM	PHILANTHROPY
LEVI	2/20 - 3/22 PISCES	MYSTIC	I BELIEVE	COMPASSION	DEVOTION	IDEALISM

Our earth and solar system is surrounded by the twelve constellations of the zodiac. It is from that "day unto day uttereth speech, and night sheweth knowledge." Our earth and solar system will be under the direct influence of the constellation Aquarius for approximately the next two thousand years. This comprises the Aquarian, or New, Age.

-Dr. Arnold Michael

LET IT

"Let it" are the words shouted by my tennis partner when he thought I might hit an out ball. In other word don't interfere with it … Let it go! Let it be.

Let It

Let Love dampen the fire of hatred

Let Peace mediate the passion for conflict

Let Joy bring happiness to sadness

Let inner Beauty burst fourth into form

Let Cooperation be the hallmark of human endeavor

Let Creativity bring fourth the fruit of the Spirit

Let Intelligence be applied to all challenges

Let Us know these resources of Being are within humanity

Let It do the work

BIBLIOGRAPHY

1. Fox, Emmet. 1993 *Diagrams For Living*, San Francisco, California, HarperSanFrancisco, 229 pages, FirstHarperCollins paperback edition.

BIOGRAPHIES

Arnold Michael, D.D., LHD, Fellow of Religious Science, author of "Blessed Among Women," "Brothers of the Grape," "The Discipline of Delight," and numerous articles, and two screen plays. "Doctor Mike" was also an outstanding teacher, counselor and minister in the field of Spiritual-Psychology in the New Thought Movement of the 20th Century. In 1970 he founded the Church of the Talking Pine as a result of a mystical experience. Through his teachings and writings, this church without walls evolved into the Madonna Ministry. Devoted to the Beloved Mother Mary since he first became acquainted with Her during the writing of Her life's story in the mid 1940s. His contemporaries like Dr. Robert Muller, Water Starcke, Fenwicke Holmes, Ernest Holmes, Starr Daily, Donald Curtis, Herman Adrian Spruit, and Archbishop Lowell Paul Wadle admired his work. Arnold drew inspiration from Mme. Lydia M. Von Finkelstein Mountford, who provided the foundation for the historical facts found in "Blessed Among Women." Mountford, a gifted historian from Israel, is the author of "Jesus Christ in His Homeland."

Charles Sommer, Fellow of Religious Science, Director Emeritus, Madonna Ministry, Director Global Citizens Publishing, Producer, Author and Writer in the field of Spiritual-Psychology, author of *Licking Your Wounds, Dynamics of Living Love and The Next Step With Spirit.*

Arnold Michael

Reverend Charles Sommer
"I look up to Arnold as I wear the cross given to
him by his mentor."

www.ingramcontent.com/pod-product-compliance
Lightning Source LLC
Chambersburg PA
CBHW021220020426
42331CB00003B/390